School Specialty.
Publishing

Copyright © 2007 School Specialty Publishing. Published by Brighter Child®, an imprint of School Specialty Publishing, a member of the School Specialty Family.

Printed in the United States of America. All rights reserved. Except as permitted under the United States Copyright Act, no part of this publication may be reproduced or distributed in any form or by any means, or stored in a database or retrieval system, without prior written permission from the publisher, unless otherwise indicated.

Send all inquiries to:
School Specialty Publishing
8720 Orion Place
Columbus, OH 43240-2111

ISBN 0-7696-4907-6

1 2 3 4 5 6 7 8 9 POH 10 09 08 07 06

Time

What is the best way to tell what time it is? Look at a clock. There are all kinds of clocks.

Directions: Circle  the ones you have seen.

Name _____

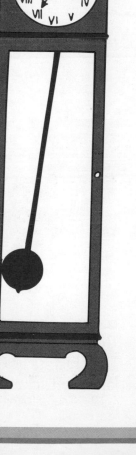

8:00

Directions: Trace  the numbers **1–12** in order on the clock.

Time

Name _____

Hickory Dickory Dock,
The mouse ran up the clock.
The clock struck one and down he ran.
Hickory Dickory Dock.

Time

A clock can tell you what time it is. A clock has different parts.

Name _____

Read and **trace** each part of the clock.

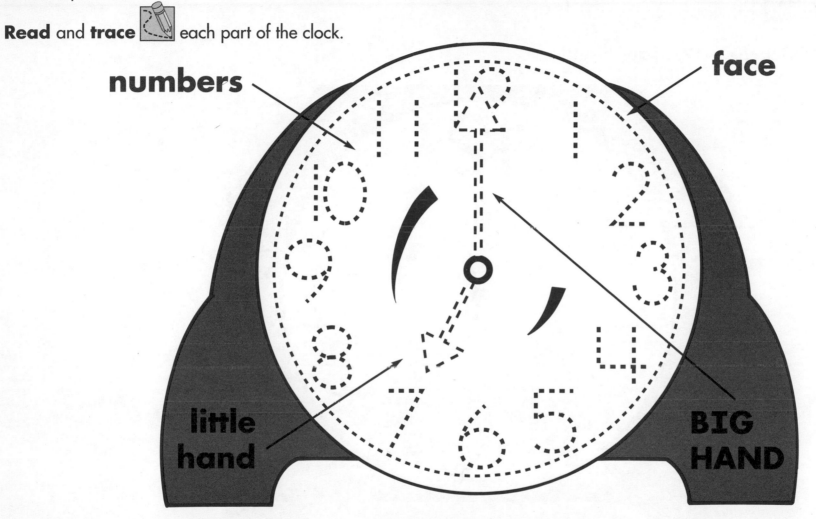

numbers

face

little hand

BIG HAND

The **BIG HAND** is on **12**.
The **little hand** tells the hour.

Name _____

A clock tells us the time.

Directions: Write  the numbers on the clock face.

Draw the **BIG HAND** to **12**. **Draw** the **little hand** to **5**.

What time is it? _____ o'clock.

Time

Directions: There are six mistakes on this clock.

Draw an **X** on each mistake.

Name _____

Time

Mrs. Murky is teaching the monsters how to tell time. She shows them this clock, which says it's **2** o'clock.

Name _____

Directions: Look at the hands on the clock. They point to numbers. One hand is longer. It's called the **big hand**. The other hand is shorter. It's called the **small hand**. We know it is 2 o'clock because the big hand is pointing to **12** and the small hand is pointing to the **2**.

Name _____

An **hour** is **sixty minutes** long.

It takes an **hour** for the
BIG HAND to go around the clock.

When the **BIG HAND** is on **12**, and the **little hand** points to a number, that is **the hour**!

The **BIG HAND** is on the **12**. Color 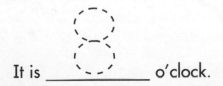 it red.
The **little hand** is on the **8**. Color it **blue**.

The **BIG HAND** is on _____.

The **little hand** is on _____.

It is _____ o'clock.

Color  the **little hour hand red**.
Fill in the blanks.

Name _____

The **BIG HAND** is on

_____.

The **little hand** is on

_____.

It is _____ o'clock.

The **BIG HAND** is on

_____.

The **little hand** is on

_____.

It is _____ o'clock.

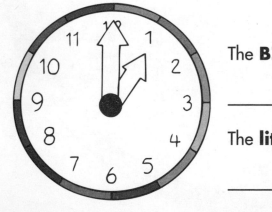

The **BIG HAND** is on

_____.

The **little hand** is on

_____.

It is _____ o'clock.

The **BIG HAND** is on

_____.

The **little hand** is on

_____.

It is _____ o'clock.

Time

Directions: Write ✏️ the time Maggie and Didi do each thing on the line beside each picture.

Name _____

_____ o'clock

_____ o'clock

_____ o'clock

_____ o'clock

Time

Maggie loves her pet, Didi. She takes care of Didi all day long.

Name _____

Directions: Write the time Maggie and Didi do each thing on the line below each picture.

_____ o'clock

_____ o'clock

Directions: Write  the time that is on each clock. The first one is done for you.

Name _____

2 _____ o'clock

_____ o'clock

_____ o'clock

_____ o'clock

Time

Milo had a very busy day. What time did he complete each thing?

Directions: Write the time for each thing on the lines beside the pictures.

Name _____

_____ o'clock

_____ o'clock

_____ o'clock

_____ o'clock

14

Time

Directions: Write  the time for each thing on the lines beside the pictures.

Name _____

_____ o'clock

_____ o'clock

_____ o'clock

Rodney had a busy day today, too.

Directions: Write  the time he did each thing on the lines below the pictures.

Name _____

_____ o'clock

_____ o'clock

Directions: Write  the time he did each thing on the lines beside the pictures.

Name _____

_____ o'clock

_____ o'clock

_____ o'clock

_____ o'clock

Time

Help the monsters tell time by completing the clocks below.

Directions: Draw  a **small hand** on each clock to show what time it is.

Name _____

1 o'clock

3 o'clock

6 o'clock

Directions: Draw  a **small hand** on each clock to show what time it is.

Name _____

8 o'clock

10 o'clock

12 o'clock

Time

If the **BIG HAND** is on **12**, it is easy to tell the time. Look and see the hour.

Name _____

Directions: Trace the **little hand** to make the hour **10 o'clock**.

The **BIG HAND** is on _____ .

The **little hand** is on _____ .

It is _____ o'clock.

Time

Directions: Draw  the **little hour hand** on each clock.

Name _____

8 o'clock.

1 o'clock.

7 o'clock.

Directions: Draw the **little hour hand** on each clock.

Name _____

2 o'clock.

10 o'clock.

9 o'clock.

Time

Directions: Draw  the **little hour hand** on each clock.

Name _____

4 o'clock.

11 o'clock.

5 o'clock.

Time

Draw the **little hour hand** on each clock.

Name _____

6 o'clock.

12 o'clock.

3 o'clock.

Directions: Circle  the **little hour hand**

on each clock. What time is it? **Write** the time below.

Name _____

_____ o'clock.

_____ o'clock.

_____ o'clock.

_____ o'clock.

_____ o'clock.

_____ o'clock.

Time

The short hand of the clock tells the hour. The long hand tells how many minutes after the hour. When the minute hand is on the **12**, it is the beginning of the hour.

Directions: Look at each clock. **Write**  the time.

Example:

_3_ o'clock

____ o'clock

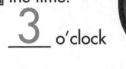

____ o'clock

____ o'clock

____ o'clock

____ o'clock

____ o'clock

____ o'clock

____ o'clock

Both clocks show the same time.

Name _____

4:00

4 o'clock
4:00

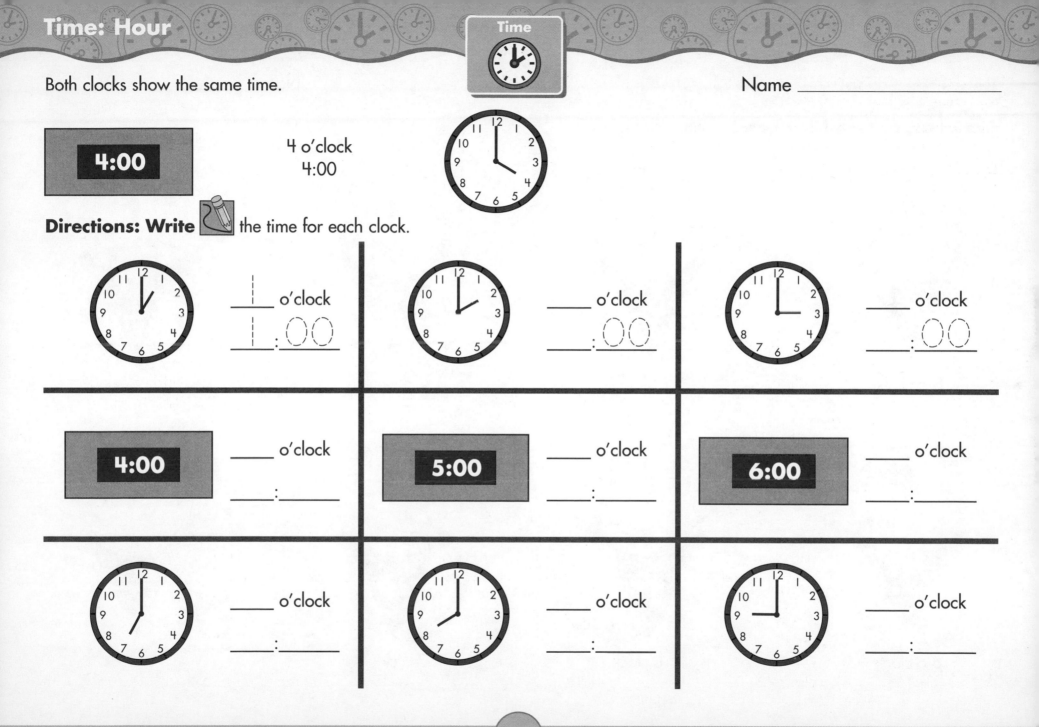

Directions: Write the time for each clock.

___4___ o'clock
__4__:00

_____ o'clock
__:00

_____ o'clock
__:00

4:00 _____ o'clock
__:_____

5:00 _____ o'clock
__:_____

6:00 _____ o'clock
__:_____

_____ o'clock
__:_____

_____ o'clock
__:_____

_____ o'clock
__:_____

Time

Name _____

Here's the Scoop!

Draw the **little hour hand** on each clock.

8 o'clock

4 o'clock

2 o'clock

1 o'clock

6 o'clock

11 o'clock

3 o'clock

5 o'clock

Time

What is the time?

Name _____

_____ o'clock

_____ o'clock

_____ o'clock

_____ o'clock

_____ o'clock

_____ o'clock

_____ o'clock

_____ o'clock

_____ o'clock

_____ o'clock

_____ o'clock

_____ o'clock

What is the time?

Name _____

_____ o'clock

_____ o'clock

_____ o'clock

_____ o'clock

_____ o'clock

_____ o'clock

_____ o'clock

_____ o'clock

_____ o'clock

Time

What is the time? It's Clown Time!

Name _____

___ o'clock

___ o'clock

___ o'clock

___ o'clock

___ o'clock

___ o'clock

___ o'clock

___ o'clock

___ o'clock

___ o'clock

___ o'clock

___ o'clock

Write ✏ the original time and **1 hour later**.

Time

Name _____

Show **1 hour later**. **Write**  the times.

Time

Name _____

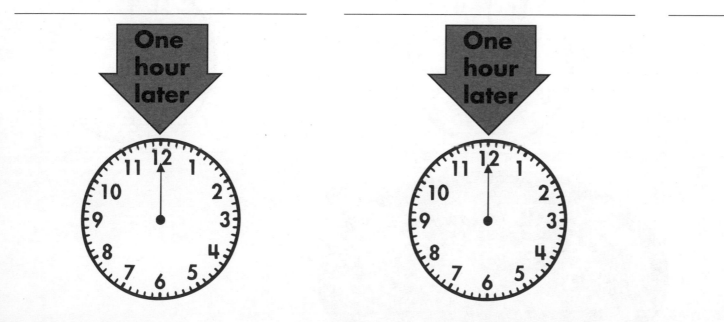

Time

Read each poem.

Draw a line to the clock that matches.

Name _____

A. It is 7 o'clock.
Time to rise and shine.
First it will rain,
Then turn out fine.

B. It is 10 o'clock.
We are at the pool.
We're happy today
Because there is no school!

C. It is 4 o'clock.
It is time to play!
We will see friends
Outside today.

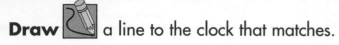

Time

Read each poem.

Draw a line to the clock that matches.

A. It is 2 o'clock.
   Now it is dark night.
   I am in bed,
   All tucked in tight.

B. It is 12 o'clock
   And time to eat.
   Have a sandwich,
   Then a treat!

C. It is 5 o'clock.
   Night is almost here.
   Evening shadows
   Are very near.

Name _____

Time

Read each poem.

Draw a line to the clock that matches.

Name _____

A. It is 8 o'clock.
   Now dinner is done.
   Time for homework
   And then some fun.

B. It is 11 o'clock,
   And I am in bed
   With a pillow
   Underneath my head.

C. It is 3 o'clock.
   We are out the door,
   To run and play,
   Then play some more.

Time

Name _____

This is a **digital clock**. It tells **time with numbers**. First, it tells the **hour**, then the **minutes**.

Draw the **little hour hand** on this face clock below to read **10 o'clock**.

Both clocks show that it is **10 o'clock**.

Make a **green** **circle** around the kinds of clocks you have at home.

Time

Trace  the time on the **digital clocks**.

Name _____

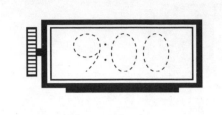

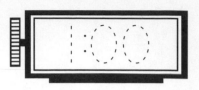

Match the clocks.

11:00

7:00

8:00

Time

Long ago, there were only **wind-up clocks**.
Today, we also have **electric** and **battery clocks**.

Name _____

Match these digital and face clocks.

Write  the time on the digital clocks.

Name _____

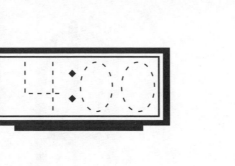

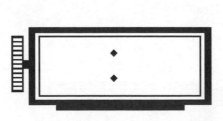

4:00

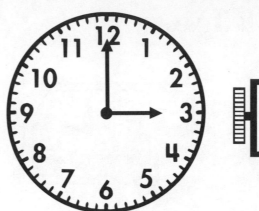

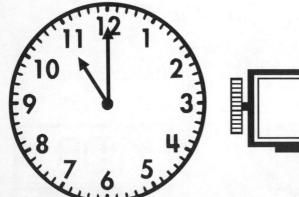

Write  the time on the digital clocks.

Time

Name _____

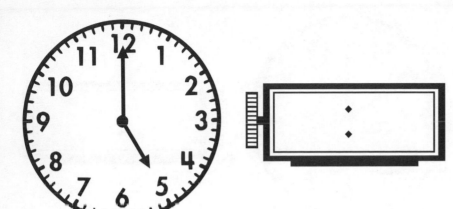

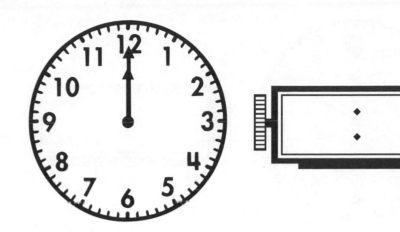

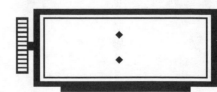

Write  the time on the digital clocks.

Time

Name _____

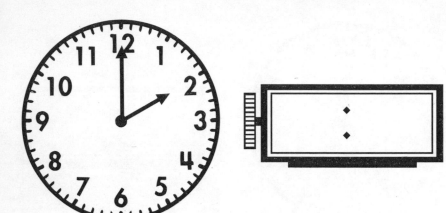

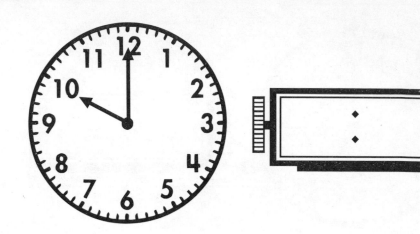

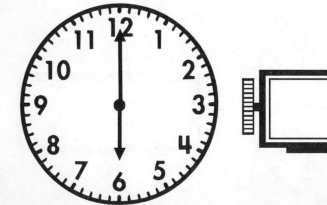

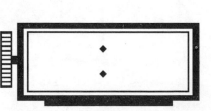

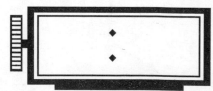

Draw the hands on each clock face.

Write the time on each digital clock.

Name _____

A. Fernando Frog eats lunch at **12 o'clock**.

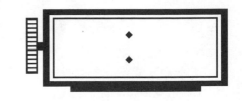

B. Fanny Frog goes to the library at **1 o'clock**.

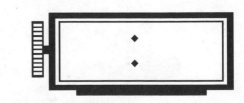

Time Two Ways

Time

Draw  the hands on each clock face.

Write the time on each digital clock.

Name _____

A. At **9 o'clock**, Frog goes for a swim.

B. At **11 o'clock**, Frog sits on a lily pad.

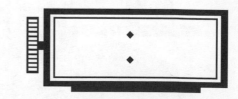

Name _____

Read each story.

Draw the hands on each clock face.

A. At **11:00**, Mouse starts to cook.
Yum-Yum! Cheese soup is good.

B. At **12 o'clock**, Mouse sets the table.
Uh–oh! He drops a spoon.

C. At **7:00**, Mouse reads a book. What a
funny story!

D. Time for bed. It is **9 o'clock**, and Mouse is
sleepy.

Time

This clock face shows the time gone by since 8 o'clock. **Thirty minutes** or **half an hour** has gone by. There are three ways to say time to the half-hour. We say **seven thirty**, **thirty minutes past seven**, or **half past seven**.

Directions: Write the times below.

Name _____

9:00 _____

9:30 _____

_____

_____

30 _____ minutes past 9 _____ o'clock

_____ minutes past _____ o'clock

46

Time

Directions: Read the time on the first clock.

Draw  hands on the second clock to show the

half hour. **Write** the times below.

Name _____

_____   _____   _____   _____

_____ minutes past _____ o'clock   _____ minutes past _____ o'clock

Directions: What is your dinner time? **Circle** the time you eat.

What time is it?

Directions: Write  the times below.

Name _____

half past _____

half past _____

half past _____

half past _____

half past _____

half past _____

Time

Who "nose" these times?

Directions: Write the time under each clock.

Color the noses.

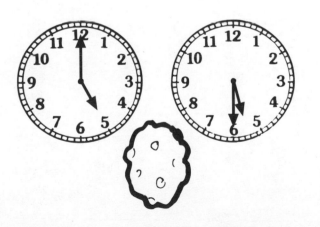

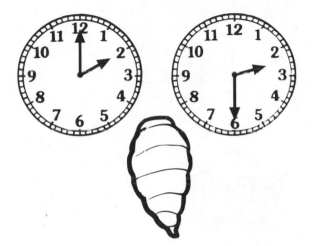

Name _____

_____   _____

_____   _____

Directions: Draw  a special watch
for yourself. Show your favorite time of day.

Name _____

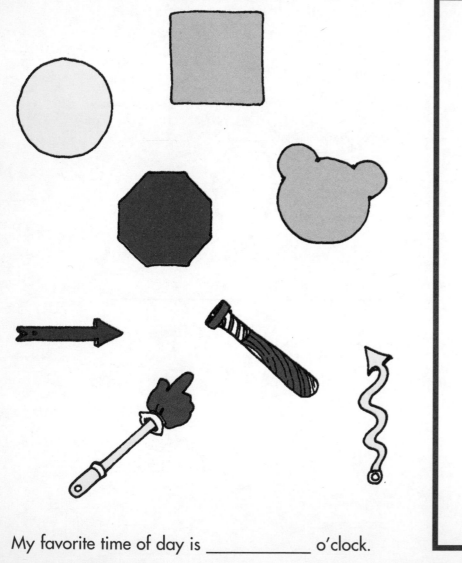

My favorite time of day is _____ o'clock.

Time

Directions: Write these important hours in your day.

Name _____

_____ o'clock

_____ :00

This is when I go to school.

_____ o'clock

_____ :00

This is when I have dinner.

_____ o'clock

_____ :00

This is when I watch my favorite TV program.

_____ o'clock

_____ :00

This is when I would <u>like</u> to go to bed.

Time

Draw a line from the clock to the correct time.

Name _____

3:00   3:30

4:00

6:30   7:00

7:30

4:00   5:00

6:00

Time

Name _____

8:00

4:30

5:00

12:00

10:30

1:00

9:30

10:30

10:00

half past _____

half past _____

Time

Space Time
What time is it?

Name _____

3:00 ____ : ____

____ : ____

____ : ____

____ : ____

____ : ____

____ : ____

____ : ____

____ : ____

____ : ____

Time

Sock Clocks

Name _____

Draw ✏️ the hands on the sock clocks.

4:30

10:00

3:30

1:30

9:30

4:00

2:30

7:00

Directions: Fill in 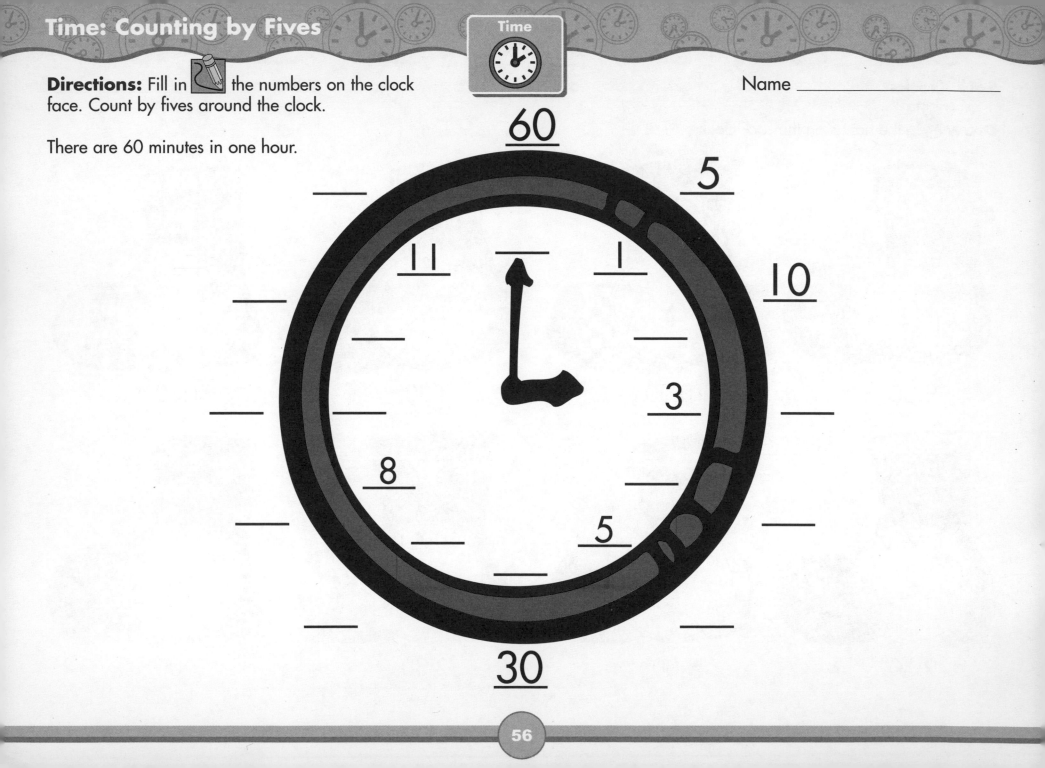 the numbers on the clock face. Count by fives around the clock.

There are 60 minutes in one hour.

Time

Name _____

60

5

11   1

10

___   ___

8   3

___   ___

5

30

56

Time on the Fives

Each **number** on the clock face stands for **5** minutes.

Name _____

Directions: Count by **5s** beginning at the **12**.

Write  the numbers below:

00 05 10 15 20 25

25

It is ___25___ minutes after ___8___ o'clock. It is written 8:25.

Directions: Count by **5s**. **Write** the numbers below.

00 ___ ___ ___ ___ ___ ___ ___

It is _____ minutes after _____ o'clock.

_____ : _____

Time

Name _____

Each **hour** has **60** minutes. An **hour** has **4 quarter-hours**. A **quarter-hour** is **15 minutes**.

This clock face shows a quarter of an hour.

From the **12** to the **3** is **15 minutes**.

From the 12 to the 3 is 15 minutes.

__15__ minutes after __8__ o'clock

is __8:15__.

Directions: Draw 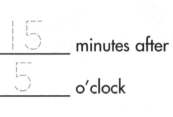 the hands. **Write** 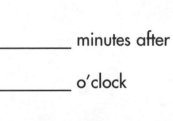 the times.

Name _____

5:15

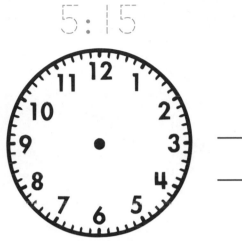

__15__ minutes after

__5__ o'clock

10:15

_____ minutes after

_____ o'clock

2:15

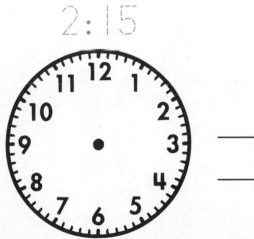

_____ minutes after

_____ o'clock

9:15

_____ minutes after

_____ o'clock

Time

Each **hour** has **4 quarter-hours**.
A **quarter-hour** is **15 minutes**.

Write the times.

Name _____

9:00

One Quarter -Hour later

9:15

_____*15*_____ minutes past _____*9*_____ o'clock

One Quarter -Hour later

_____

_____

_____ minutes past _____ o'clock

Time

Draw the hands. **Write** the times.

Name _____

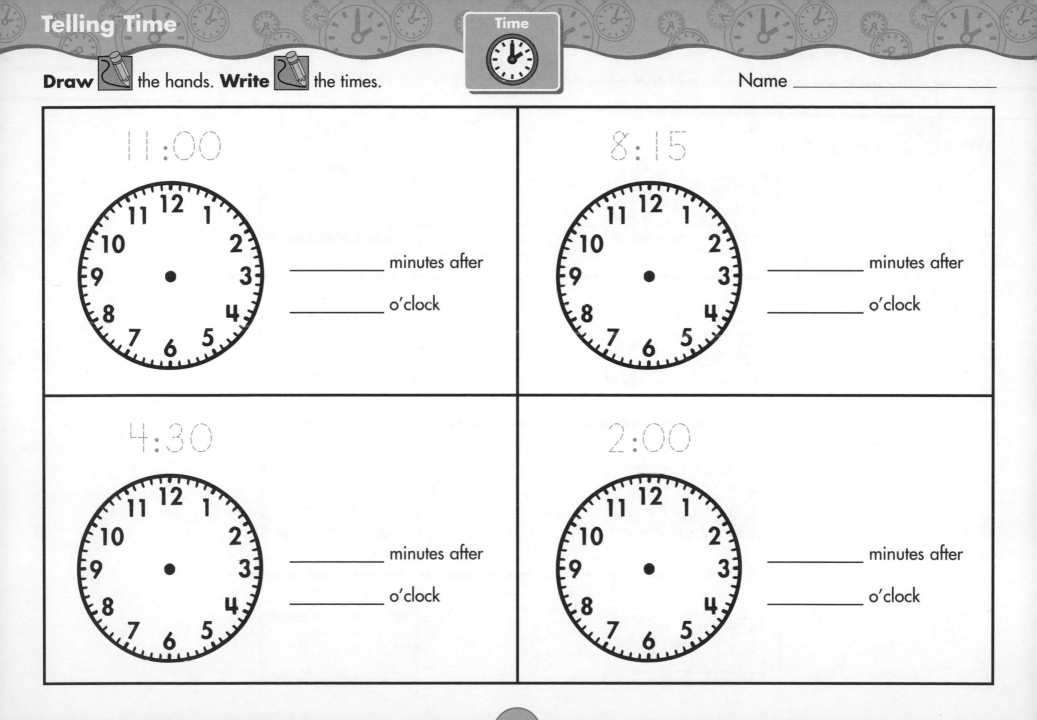

11:00

_____ minutes after

_____ o'clock

8:15

_____ minutes after

_____ o'clock

4:30

_____ minutes after

_____ o'clock

2:00

_____ minutes after

_____ o'clock

Digital Clocks

Your **digital clock** has quarter-hours, too! It also shows **15 minutes**.

Name _____

Write 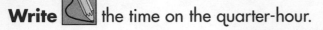 the time on the quarter-hour.

Drawing the Minute Hand

Directions: Draw the hands on these fish clocks.

Name _____

7:45

8:05

11:15

12:10

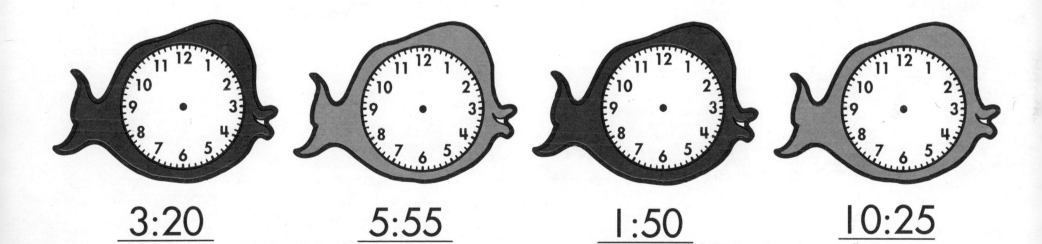

3:20

5:55

1:50

10:25

Money

Name _____

Hi! I am Mary Money.

It is important to learn about **money**.

This is a **penny**.

It is worth **1 cent**. It has **2 sides**.

front   back

This is the **cent symbol**. **Trace** it.

¢

_____

Color the pennies **brown**.

Money

A penny is worth **1** cent.

Name _____

Directions: Find each penny. **Color** it **brown**.

How many pennies did you find? _____

Money

Count the pennies.

Name _____

Directions: Write 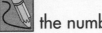 the number of cents in the blanks below.

____3____ pennies = ____3____ ¢   _____ penny = _____ ¢

_____ pennies = _____ ¢

Money

How much money is in the purse?

Name _____

Directions: Circle  the number that shows
how many cents are in each purse.

2¢

3¢

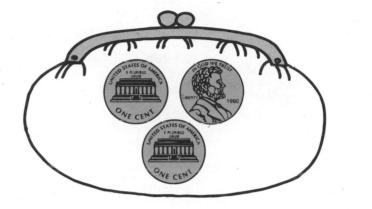

2¢

3¢

4¢

5¢

6¢

7¢

A penny is worth **1¢**. It is brown.

Money

Name _____

Directions: Circle  the correct amount of money in each row below. The first one is done for you.

1¢ (2¢) 3¢

(1¢) (2¢) 3¢

5¢ (6¢) 7¢

7¢ 8¢ (9¢)

68

Directions: Circle  the correct amount of money in each row below.

 Money

Name _____

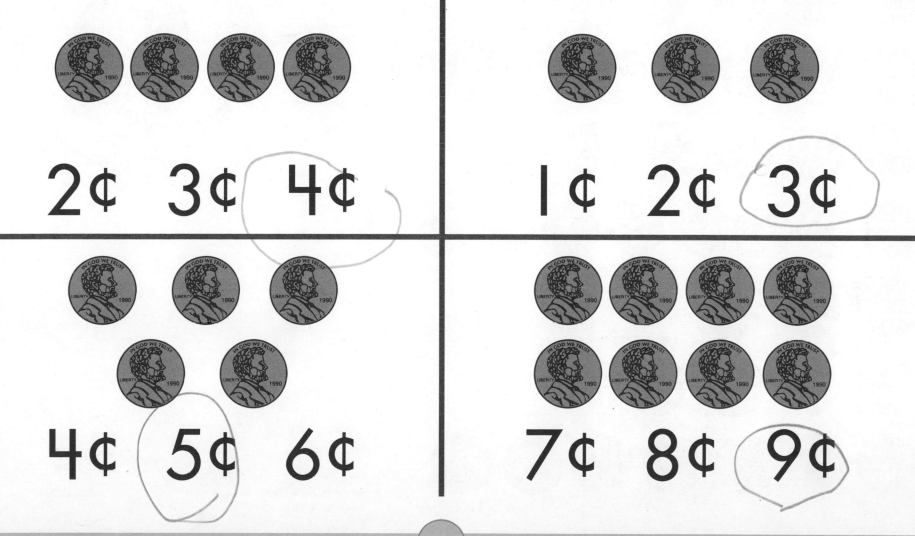

2¢   3¢   4¢

1¢   2¢   3¢

4¢   5¢   6¢

7¢   8¢   9¢

Money

Directions: Count the pennies. How many cents?

Name _____

Example:

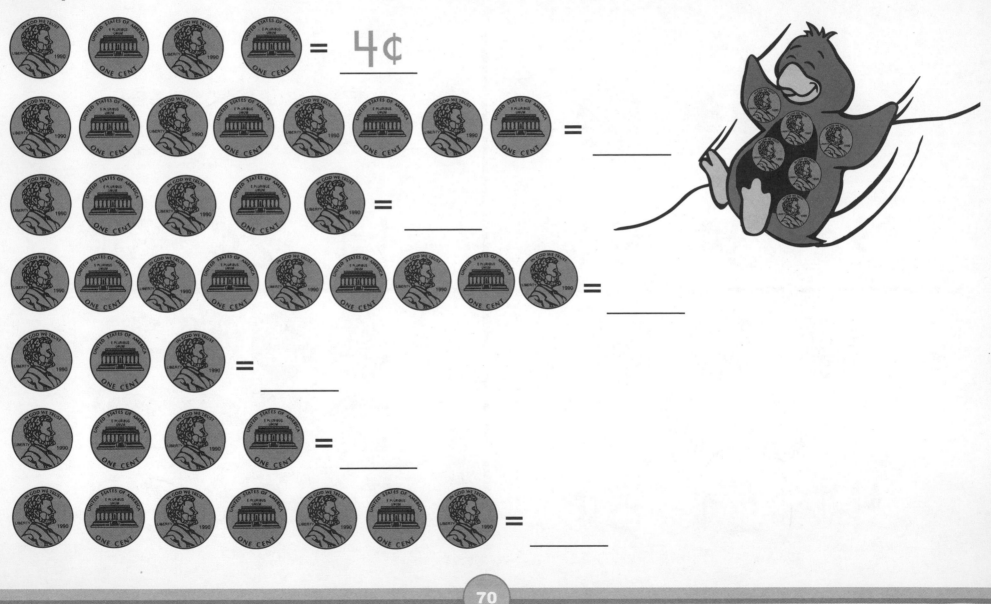

= 4¢

= _____

= _____

= _____

= _____

= _____

= _____

Penny Pinchers

Directions: Draw  a line from the pennies to the correct numbers.

Name _____

Example:

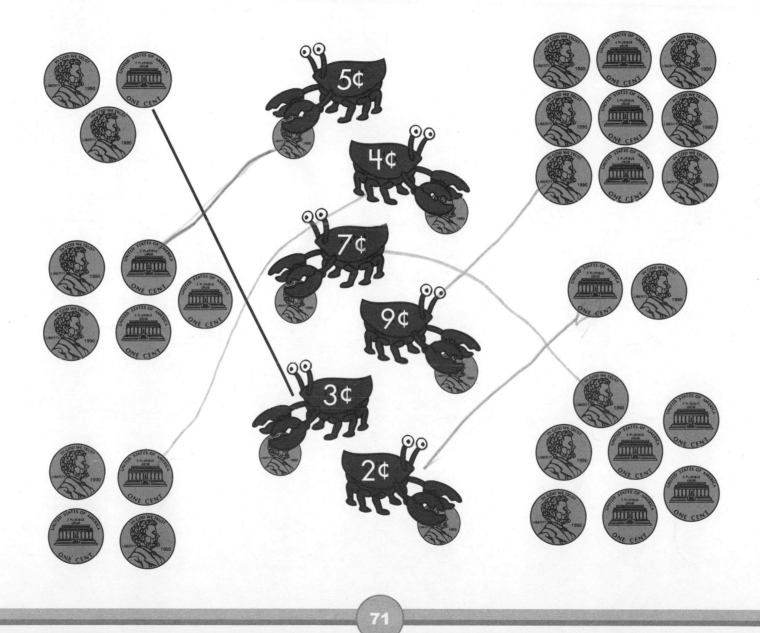

Money

Directions: Count the pennies in each triangle.

Name _____

_____ ¢   _____ ¢   _____ ¢

Money

This is a **nickel**.
It is worth **5** cents.

It has 2 sides.

front   back

Name _____

Directions: Color 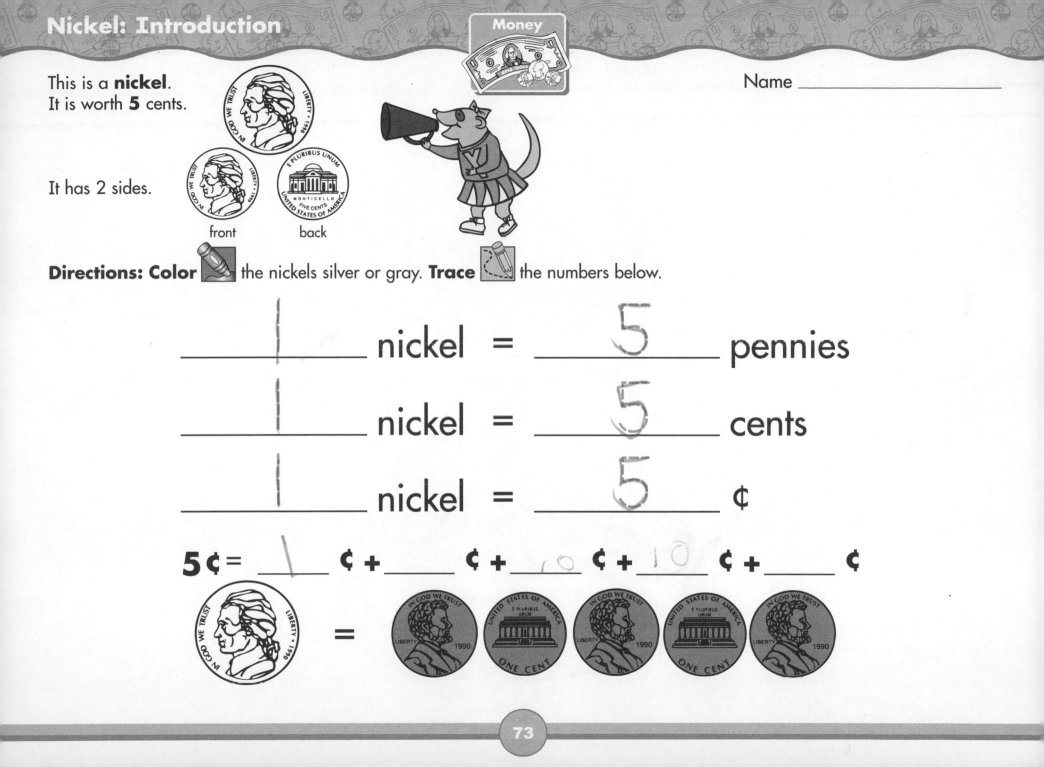 the nickels silver or gray. **Trace** the numbers below.

__1__ nickel = __5__ pennies

__1__ nickel = __5__ cents

__1__ nickel = __5__ ¢

5 ¢ = __1__ ¢ + ___ ¢ + __o__ ¢ + __10__ ¢ + ___ ¢

Money

A **nickel** is worth **5¢**. **Count** the money.

How much?

Name _____

A.

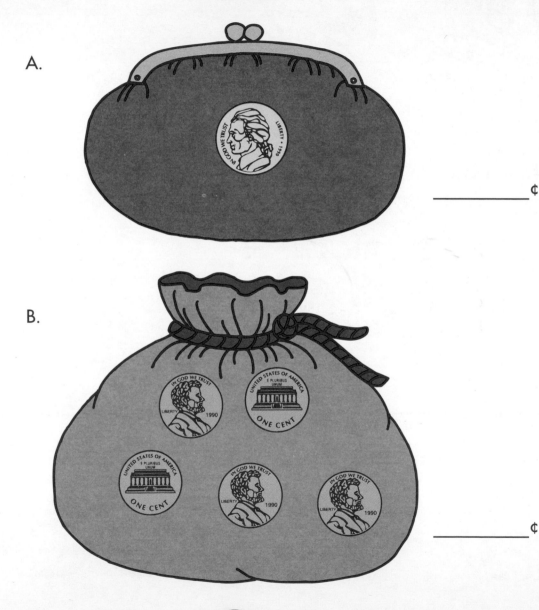

_____ ¢

B.

_____ ¢

 **Money**

Name _____

Here is a **penny**.

Color  it **brown**.

And here is a **nickel**.

Color  it silver.

I penny = _____ cent

I penny = _____ ¢

I nickel = _____ cents

I nickel = _____ ¢

Make the cent symbol here: _____

Money

A penny is worth one cent. It is written **1¢** or **$.01**.
A nickel is worth five cents. It is written **5¢** or **$.05**.

Name _____

Directions: Count the money and **write** how many cents there are.

penny   1 penny = 1¢

nickel   1 nickel = 5¢

 = __3__ ¢

 = __15__ ¢

 = _____ ¢

 = _____ ¢

 = _____ ¢

 = _____ ¢

Money

Directions: Count the money. Begin by saying
5 for the nickel and add **1** for each penny.

Name _____

= _____ ¢

= _____ ¢

= _____ ¢

= _____ ¢

Money

Directions: Count the money. Begin with the nickel. Then, count the pennies.

Write  the amount.

= _____ ¢

= _____ ¢

= _____ ¢

= _____ ¢

= _____ ¢

Money

Let's count my nickels to see if we have enough to buy something!

Name _____

Count by 5s.

See how far you can count.

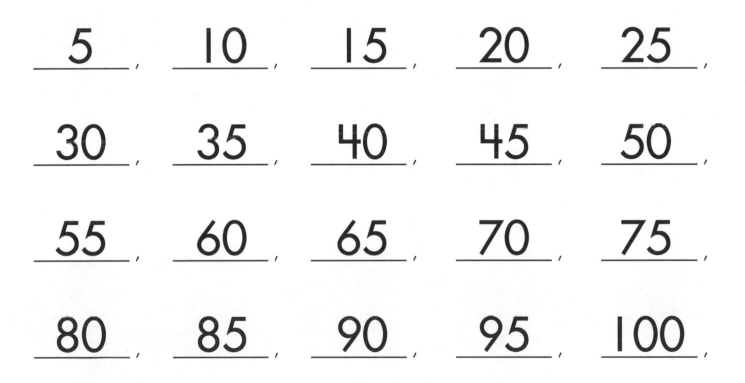

5 , 10 , 15 , 20 , 25 ,

30 , 35 , 40 , 45 , 50 ,

55 , 60 , 65 , 70 , 75 ,

80 , 85 , 90 , 95 , 100 ,

This is how to count nickels!
Practice counting by 5s!

Money

Count the nickels by 5s.

5 cents = 1 nickel

Write ✏ the amount.
Example:

Name _____

 **15** ¢

Count __5__, __10__, __15__.

 ☐ ¢

Count _____, _____.

☐ ¢

Count _____, _____, _____,

_____, _____, _____.

☐ ¢

Count _____, _____, _____,

_____, _____.

☐ ¢

Count _____, _____, _____, _____,

_____, _____, _____.

☐ ¢

Count _____, _____,

_____, _____.

Directions: Count the nickels. **Write**  the amount of money in each meter.

Example:

20¢

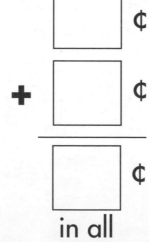

Adding With Nick and Penny

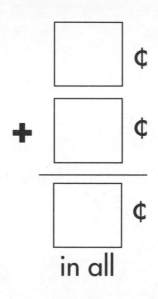

Directions: Write how much money there is in all.

Name _____

PENNY

□ ¢

+ □ ¢
_____
□ ¢

in all

□ ¢

+ □ ¢
_____
□ ¢

in all

NICK

□ ¢

+ □ ¢
_____
□ ¢

in all

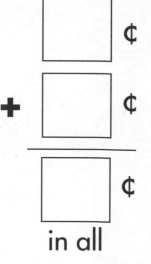

Dimes: Introduction

A dime is small, but it can buy more than a penny or a nickel.

front   back

Name _____

Each side of a dime is different. It has ridges around its edge. **Directions: Color** the dime **silver**.

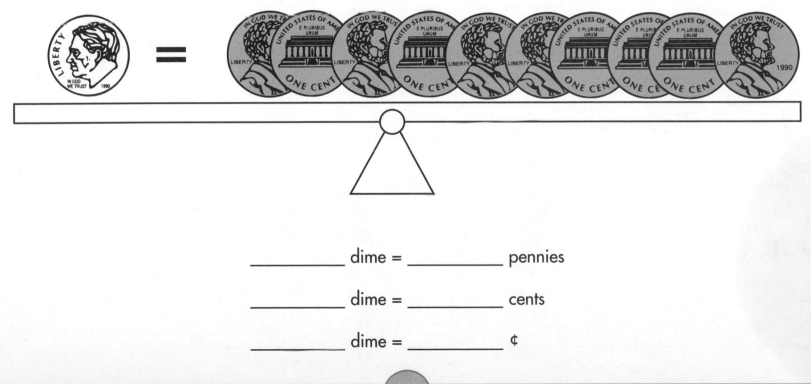

_____ dime = _____ pennies

_____ dime = _____ cents

_____ dime = _____ ¢

Money

Name _____

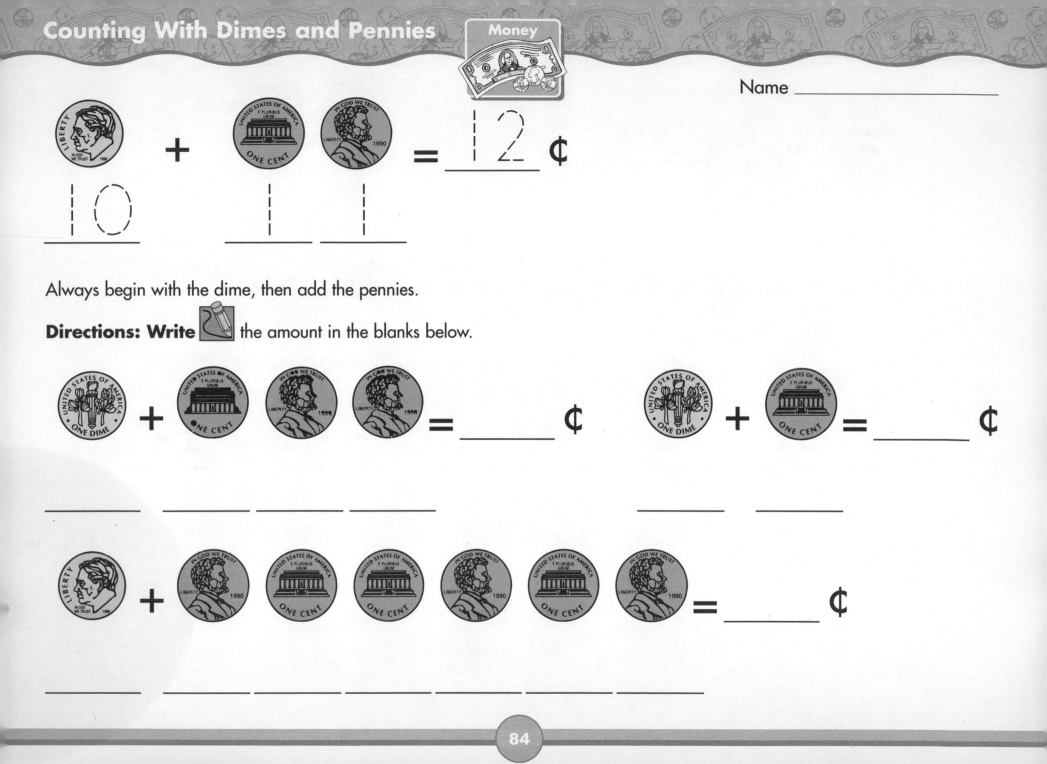

+ = __12__ ¢

10 ___ ___

Always begin with the dime, then add the pennies.

Directions: Write the amount in the blanks below.

+ = _____ ¢   + = _____ ¢

____ ____   ____ ____

+ = _____ ¢

____ ____

Money

Directions: Count the money.

Write 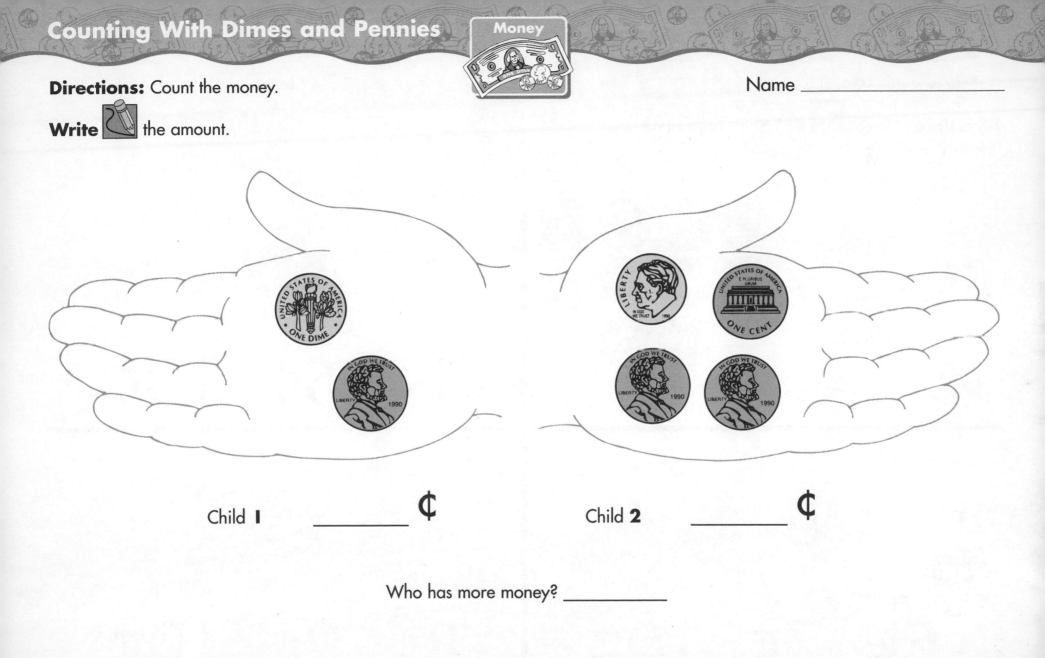 the amount.

Name _____

Child **1** _____ ¢

Child **2** _____ ¢

Who has more money? _____

Money

A dime is worth **10¢**. It is silver.

Name _____

Directions: Circle 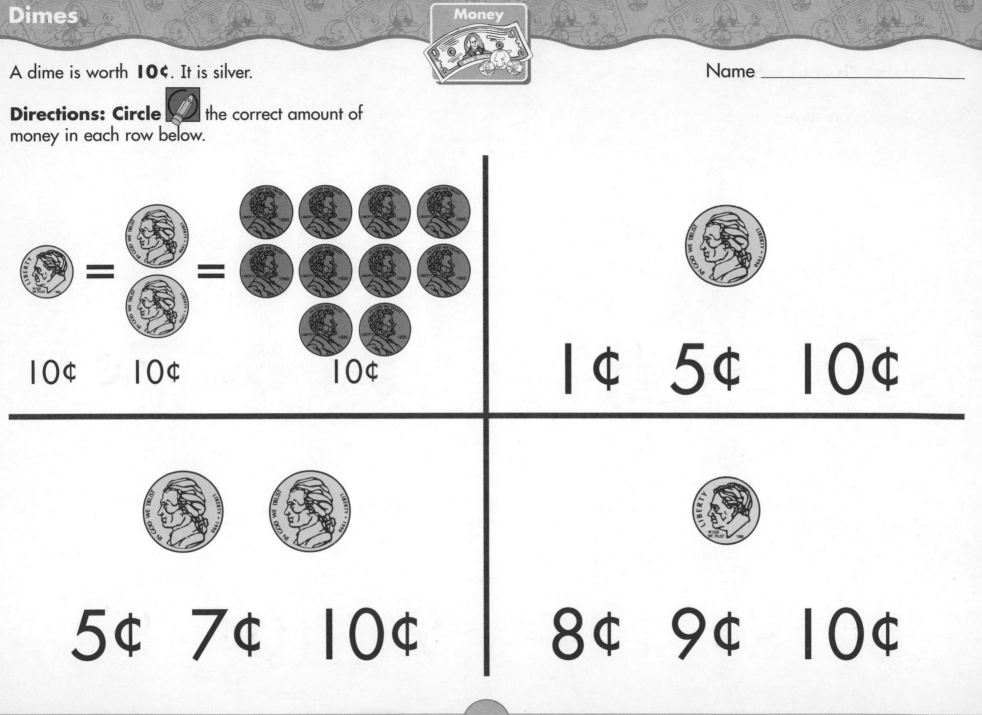 the correct amount of money in each row below.

10¢   10¢   10¢

1¢   5¢   10¢

5¢ 7¢ 10¢

8¢ 9¢ 10¢

Dimes, Nickels, Pennies

Directions: Circle the correct amount of money in each row below.

Name _____

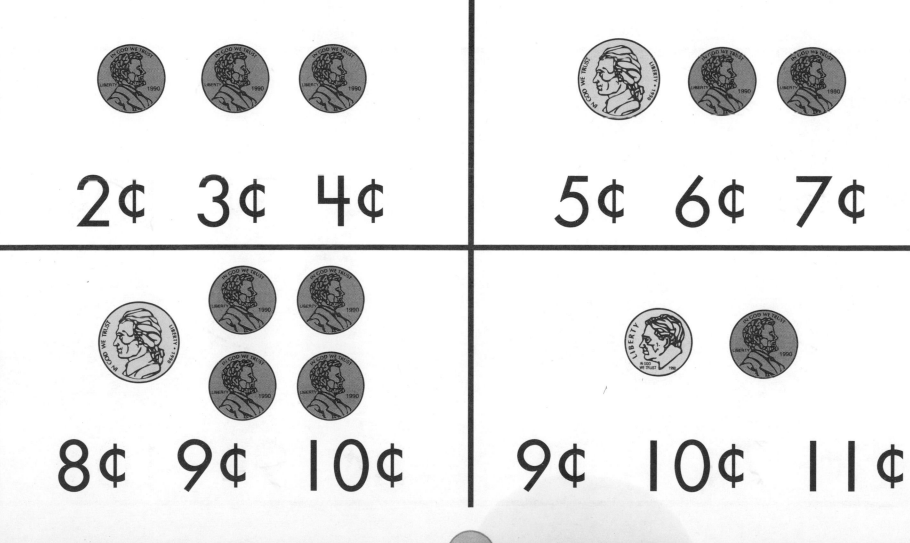

2¢   3¢   4¢

5¢   6¢   7¢

8¢   9¢   10¢

9¢   10¢   11¢

Penny, Nickel, Dime

Directions: Color each penny brown.

Draw a line under each nickel.

Draw a **circle** around each dime.

Name

penny   nickel   dime

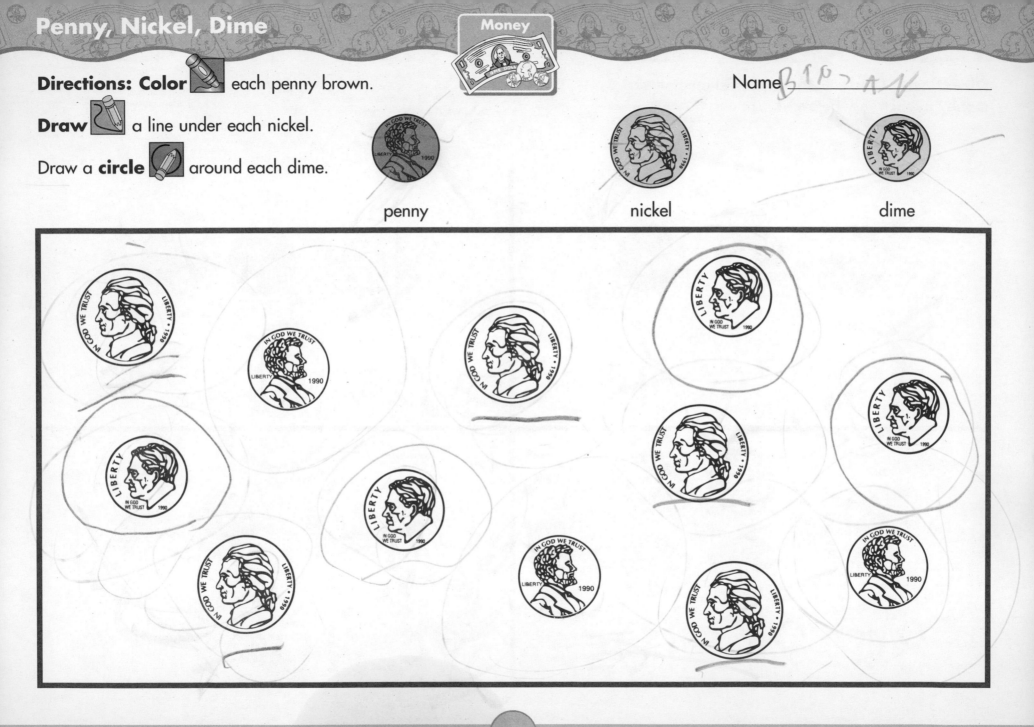

Dimes: Counting by Tens

Money

Directions: Count by 10s. Write the number.
Circle the group with more.

Name _____

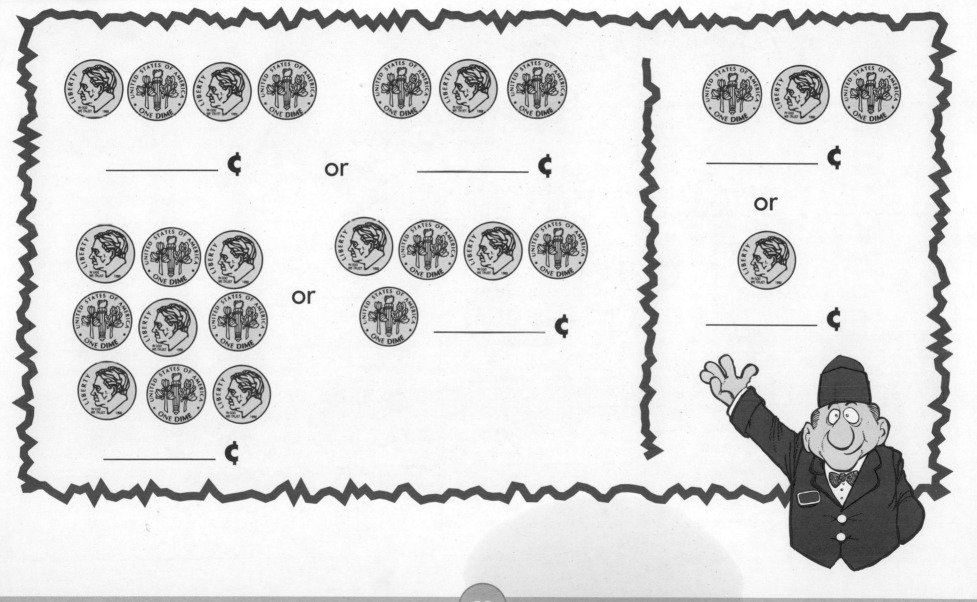

_____ ¢   or   _____ ¢

_____ ¢

or

_____ ¢

or

_____ ¢

_____ ¢

89

Count by 10s.

Name _____

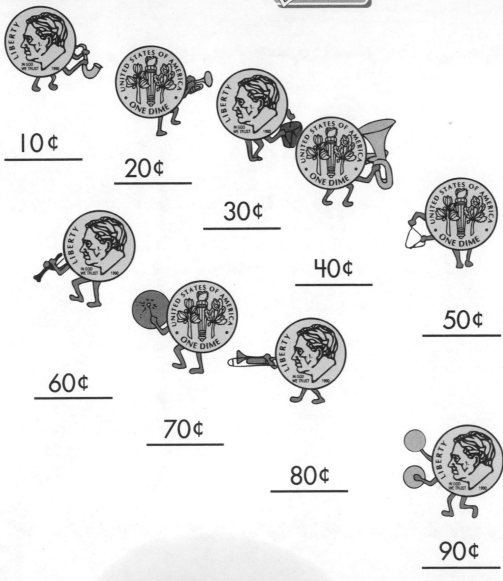

10¢ _____

20¢ _____

30¢ _____

40¢ _____

50¢ _____

60¢ _____

70¢ _____

80¢ _____

90¢ _____

100¢ _____

Counting With Dimes and Nickels

Money

Look carefully at these dimes and nickels.

Circle  two nickels, then two more, until all the nickels are circled.

Then **count** by 10s to see how much money is here.

Name _____

I see ___15___ ¢

91

Money

Count the money.

Write 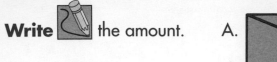 the amount.

Name _____

A.

_____ ¢

B.

_____ ¢

If you put a dime in the gumball machine, you will get three pieces of gum.

Name _____

How many pieces of gum will you get for **30** cents?

Circle your answer.

| 0 | 3 | 6 | 9 | 12 |

How much will **12** pieces of gum cost? **Circle** your answer.

20¢   40¢   60¢   80¢   100¢

Name _____

Cosmos is selling lemonade. The other monsters want to buy some. The lemonade costs **10¢**, or **10 pennies**. Do the monsters have enough money to buy lemonade? Read the clues below to find out.

Directions: Write  your answers on the lines. A nickel is the same as **5** pennies.

Hugh has **4** pennies and **1** nickel.
How much more money does he need?

_____

Rimsley has **6** pennies.
How much more money does he need?

_____

Ursula has **2** pennies and **1** nickel.
How much more money does she need?

_____

Money

Count the money.

Name _____

Start with dimes. Then count the nickels and pennies.

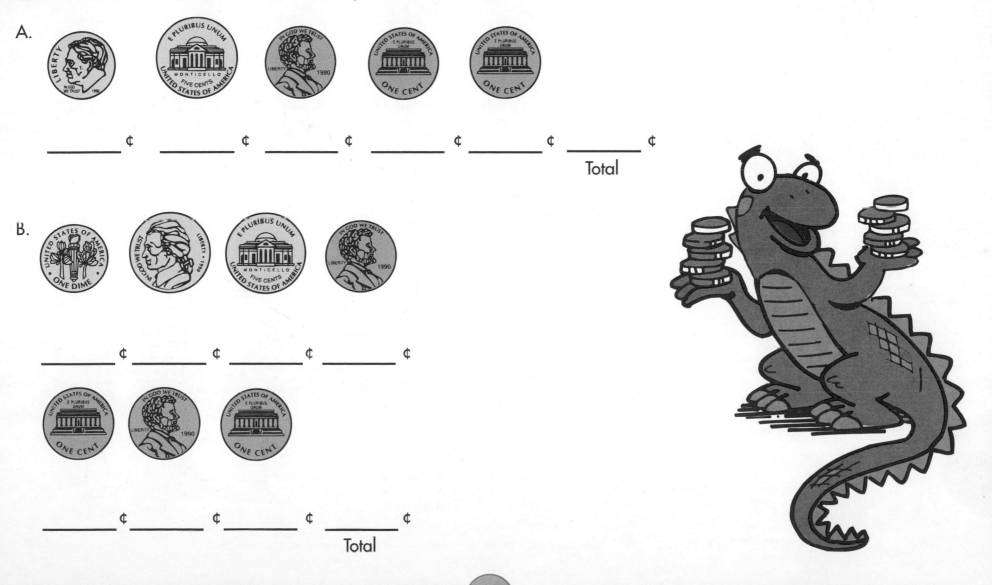

A.

_____ ¢   _____ ¢   _____ ¢   _____ ¢   _____ ¢   _____ ¢

Total

B.

_____ ¢   _____ ¢   _____ ¢   _____ ¢

_____ ¢   _____ ¢   _____ ¢   _____ ¢

Total

Money

Our first president, George Washington, is on the front. The American eagle is on the back.

Name _____

front   back

Directions: Write the number of cents in a quarter.

_____ quarter = _____ pennies

_____ quarter = _____ cents

_____ quarter = _____ ¢

Directions: Count these nickels by 5s. Is this another way to make 25¢?

yes   no

Follow each path to see how many quarters Mike and Maria found.

The **bananas** cost **25¢** each. How many can they buy?

Maria found quarters to buy

_____5_____ bananas.

Mike found quarters to buy

_____3_____ bananas.

Name _BIPZAN_

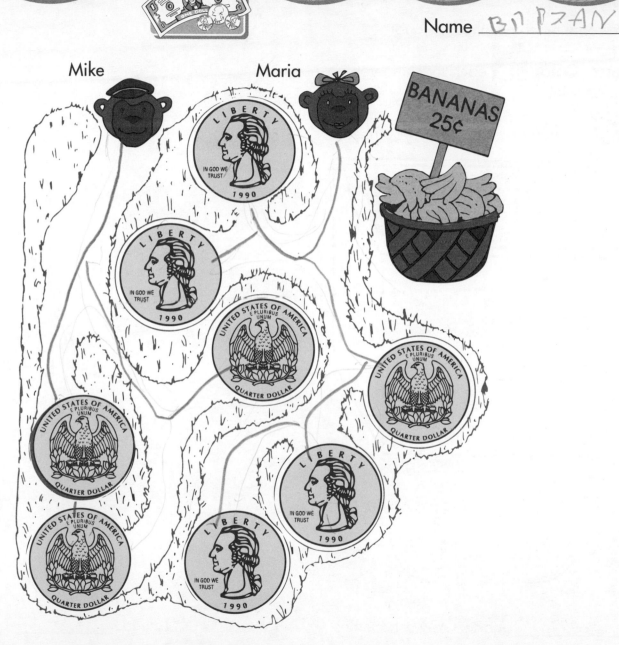

Mike   Maria

BANANAS 25¢

Money

Name _____

These are some machines that use quarters.

Directions: Color  each machine you have to put quarters into.

Circle the number of quarters you need.

I need _____ quarters to wash clothes.

I need _____ quarter(s) to make a phone call.

Money

These are all ways to make **25¢**.

Color  each coin.

Name _____

2 dimes,
1 nickel

25 pennies

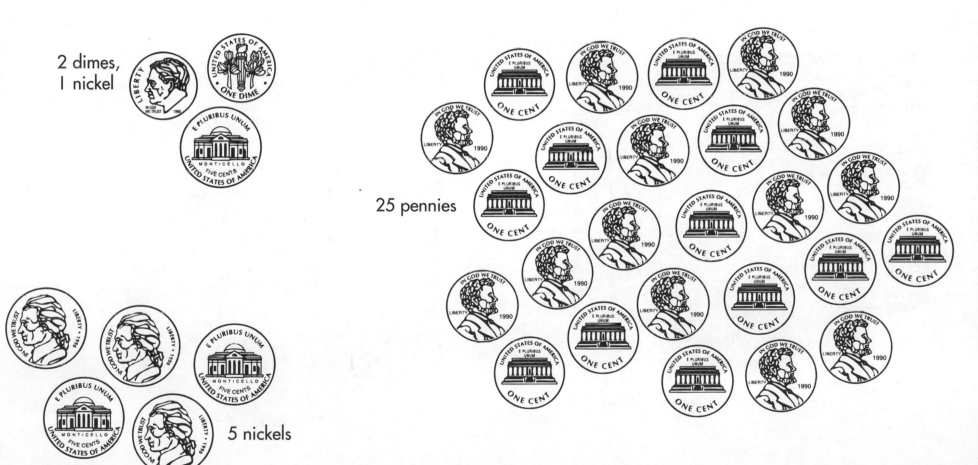

5 nickels

Money

Count the money.

Write  the amount.

A quarter is worth **25¢**.

Both of these pockets **show 25¢**.

Name _____

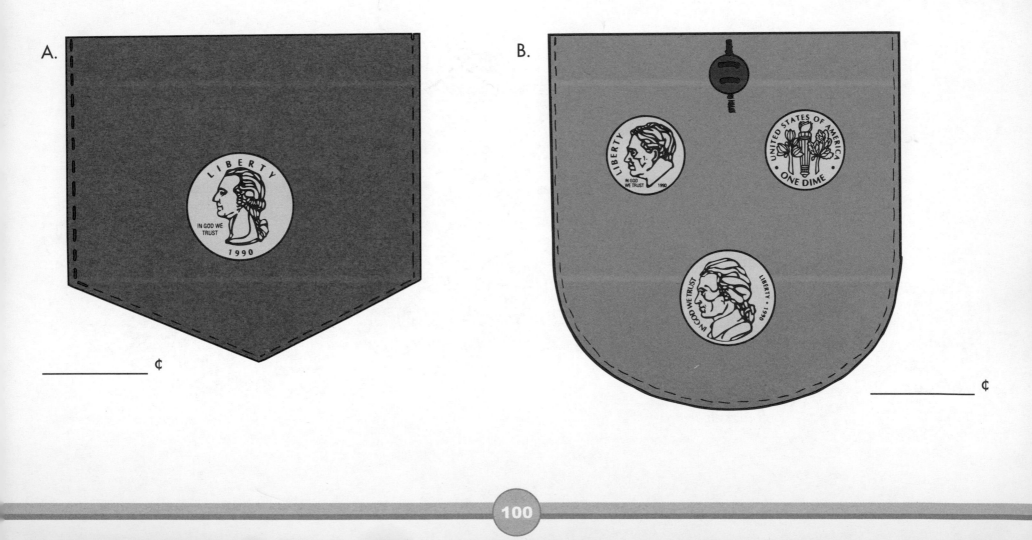

A.

_____ ¢

B.

_____ ¢

Money

Name _____

The children had fun spending the allowance they earned. The boys bought some cars.

Terry paid 5¢ for each **blue** car.

Color  Terry's cars **blue**.

5¢ each

How much did Terry pay for the **blue** cars? _____ ¢

Lucas liked the **red** cars. They were the same price. **Color** his cars **red**.

5¢ each

How much did Lucas pay for the **red** cars? _____ ¢

Which boy paid more? _____

Directions: Match the money with the amount.

Name _____

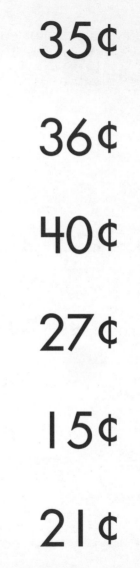

35¢

36¢

40¢

27¢

15¢

21¢

Money

Here are things to buy for your hair.

Name _____

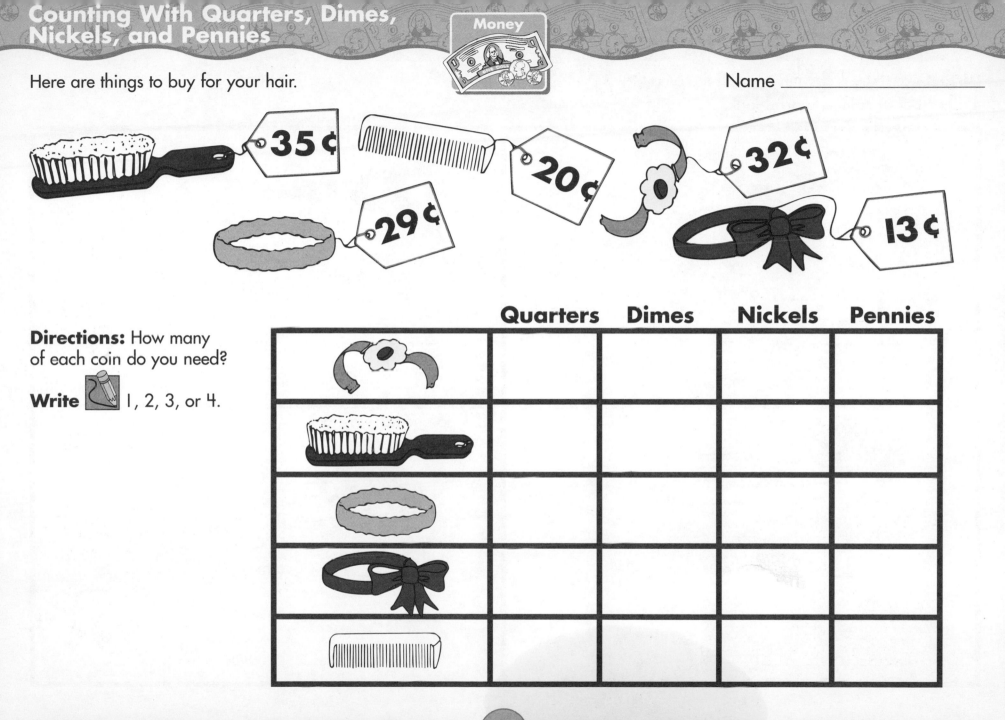

35¢

20¢

32¢

29¢

13¢

Directions: How many of each coin do you need?

Write 1, 2, 3, or 4.

		Quarters	Dimes	Nickels	Pennies

Problem Solving With Money

Directions: Draw the coins you use. **Write** the number of coins in each blank.

Name _____

1.

9¢

_____ dimes

_____ nickels

_____ pennies

2.

11¢

_____ dimes

_____ nickels

_____ pennies

3.

14¢

_____ dimes

_____ nickels

_____ pennies

4. Find another way to pay for the

14¢

_____ dimes

_____ nickels

_____ pennies

Problem Solving With Money

Directions: Draw the coins you use. **Write** the number of coins in each blank.

Name _____

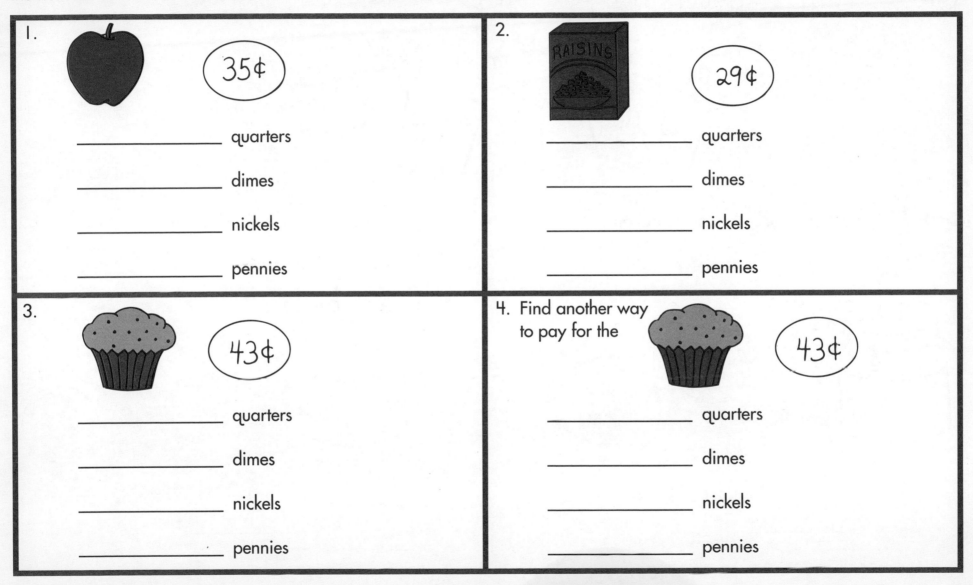

1. 35¢

_____ quarters

_____ dimes

_____ nickels

_____ pennies

2. RAISINS 29¢

_____ quarters

_____ dimes

_____ nickels

_____ pennies

3. 43¢

_____ quarters

_____ dimes

_____ nickels

_____ pennies

4. Find another way to pay for the   43¢

_____ quarters

_____ dimes

_____ nickels

_____ pennies

(Use with page 107)
Christopher was a good shopper. He looked for the best prices when he bought school supplies.

Name _____

30¢   25¢

Circle and **color** the one he bought.

   or

_____ ¢   _____ ¢

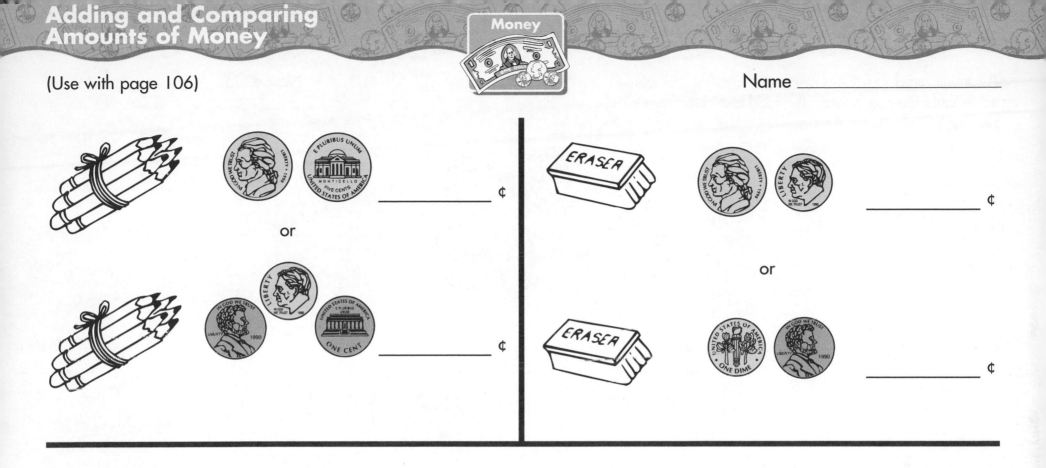

Money

Name _____

_____ ¢

or

_____ ¢

ERASER   _____ ¢

or

ERASER   _____ ¢

Draw the coins you think he spent for this notebook. Good job, Chris! **Spend wisely!**

How much? _____ ¢

Money

Adam wanted to know how much change he would have left when he bought things. He made this picture to help him subtract.

4 dimes
− 1 dime
―――――
3 dimes

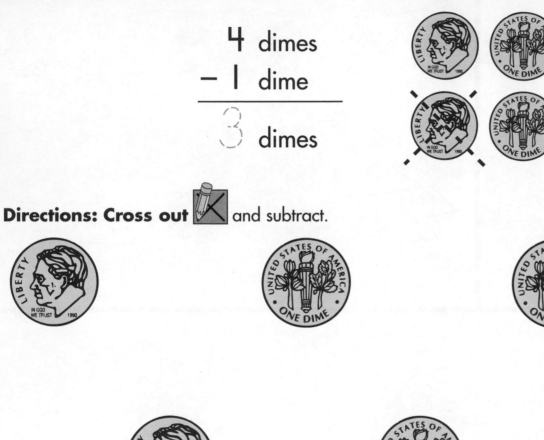

40 ¢
− 10 ¢
―――――
30 ¢

Name _____

Directions: Cross out **and subtract.**

6 dimes
− 4 dimes
―――――――

dimes

60 ¢
− 40 ¢
―――――

¢

Subtracting for Change

Pay the exact amount for each toy.

Cross out ✗ the coins you use. **How much is left?**

Name _____

A.
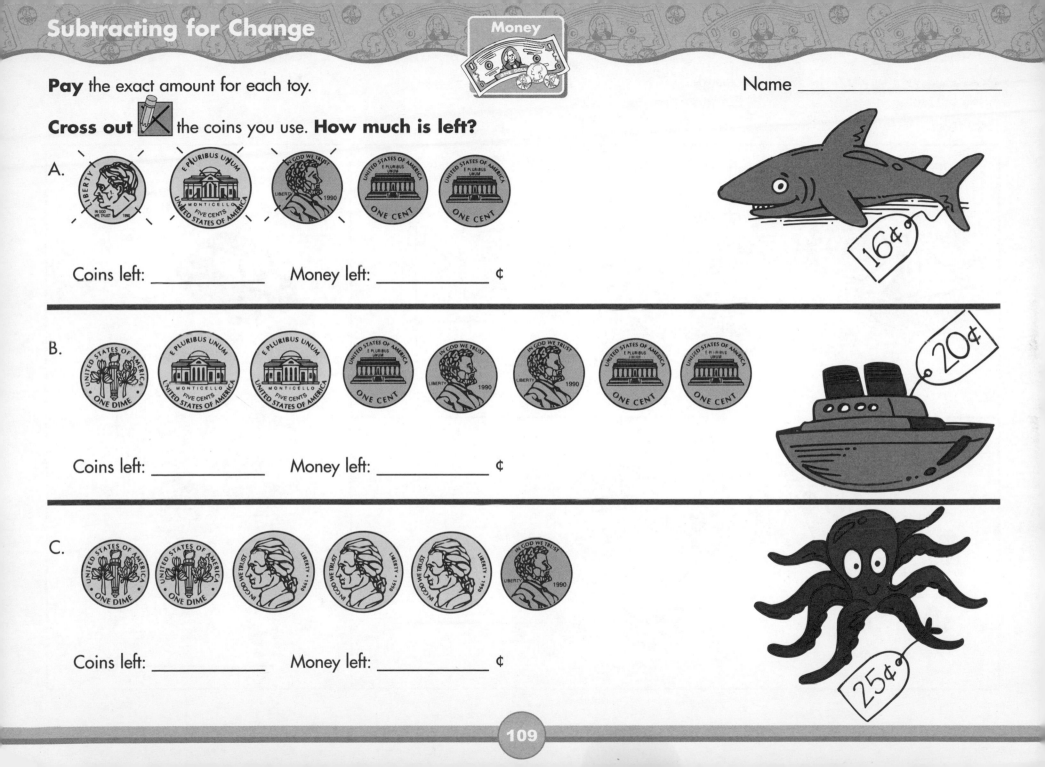

Coins left: _____ Money left: _____ ¢

B.

Coins left: _____ Money left: _____ ¢

C.

Coins left: _____ Money left: _____ ¢

16¢

20¢

25¢

Cross out ✗. **Write** ✍ the problem.

Name _____

Example:

Adam wants:

60¢

Adam has:

$$
\begin{array}{r}
65¢ \\
-\ 60¢ \\
\hline
5¢
\end{array}
$$

Adam wants:

60¢

Adam has:

_____ ¢

−_____ ¢
_____

Adam wants:

45¢

Adam has:

_____ ¢

−_____ ¢
_____

Money

Maria went to the store to buy a birthday gift for her best friend.

Maria took 50¢ to the store. She looked at these things.

Circle the things she could buy.

29¢

16¢

32¢

65¢

36¢

Name _____

Money

Maria wanted to know how much change she would get back from each toy.

Color the toy you think Maria chose.

Name _____

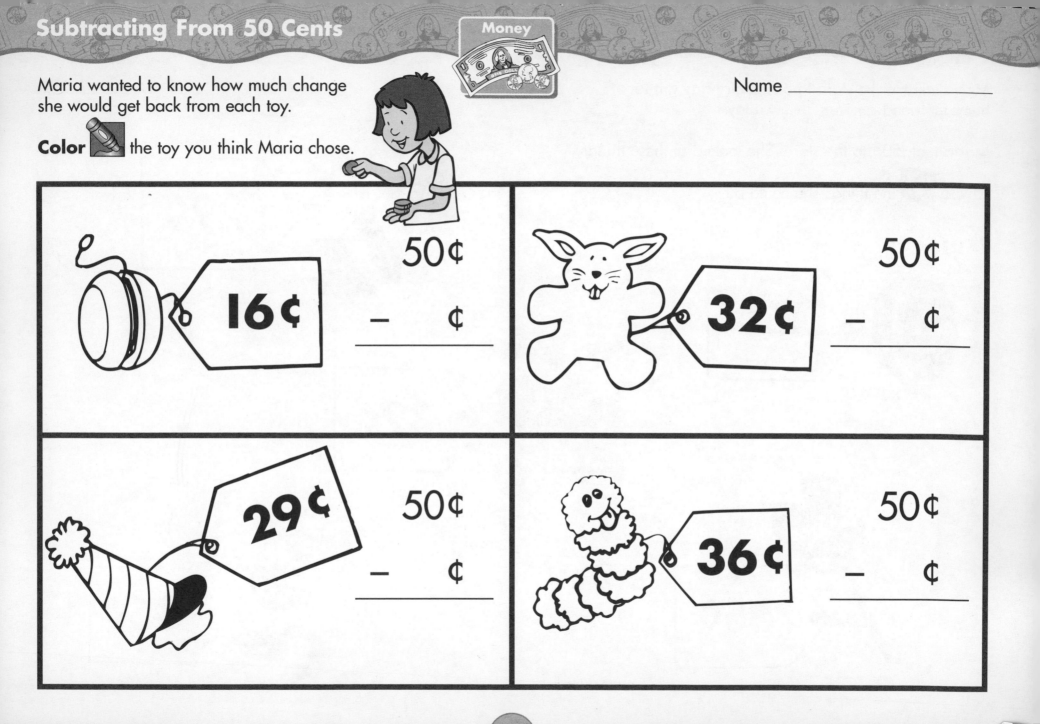

50¢

16¢

− ____ ¢

_____

50¢

32¢

− ____ ¢

_____

29¢

50¢

− ____ ¢

_____

50¢

36¢

− ____ ¢

_____

Use dimes, nickels, and pennies.
Pay the exact amount for each toy.

Name _____

A. What coins did you use?

_____ dimes

_____ nickels

_____ pennies

B. What coins did you use?

_____ dimes

_____ nickels

_____ pennies

C. What coins did Cat use to pay for the ball?

_____ dimes

_____ nickels

_____ pennies

Money

Use quarters, dimes, nickels, and pennies.
Pay the exact amount for each toy.

Name _____

I used 4 coins to pay.

A. What coins did you use?

_____ quarters

_____ dimes

_____ nickels

_____ pennies

B. What coins did you use?

_____ quarters

_____ dimes

_____ nickels

_____ pennies

C. **Solve** this puzzle.

What coins did Frog use to pay for the bow tie?

_____ quarters

_____ dimes

_____ nickels

_____ pennies

Money

Name _____

Use the coins shown.
Pay the exact amount for each toy.
How much do you have left?

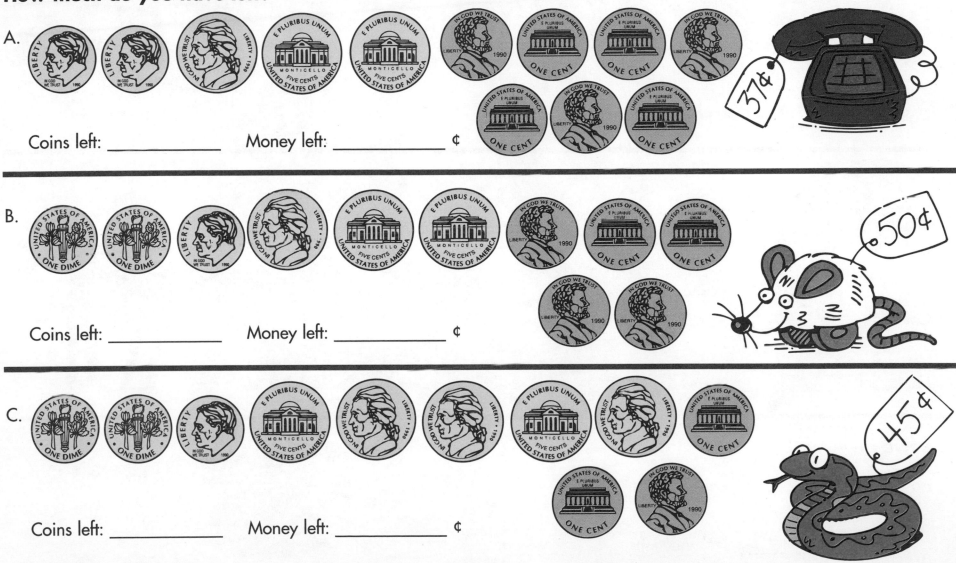

A.   37¢

Coins left: _____   Money left: _____ ¢

B.   50¢

Coins left: _____   Money left: _____ ¢

C.   45¢

Coins left: _____   Money left: _____ ¢

Money

Use the coins shown.
Pay the exact amount for each toy.

Name _____

A.

80¢

Coins left: _____   Money left: _____ ¢

B.

75¢

Coins left: _____

Money left: _____ ¢

C. **Solve** this puzzle.

60¢

How much money does Squirrel have left?

I had 2 quarters, 3 dimes, and 1 nickel. I paid for the sunglasses. Now I have one coin left.

Coins left: _____   Money left: _____ ¢

Problem Solving With Money

Directions: Draw the coins you use. Write the number of coins in each blank.

Name _____

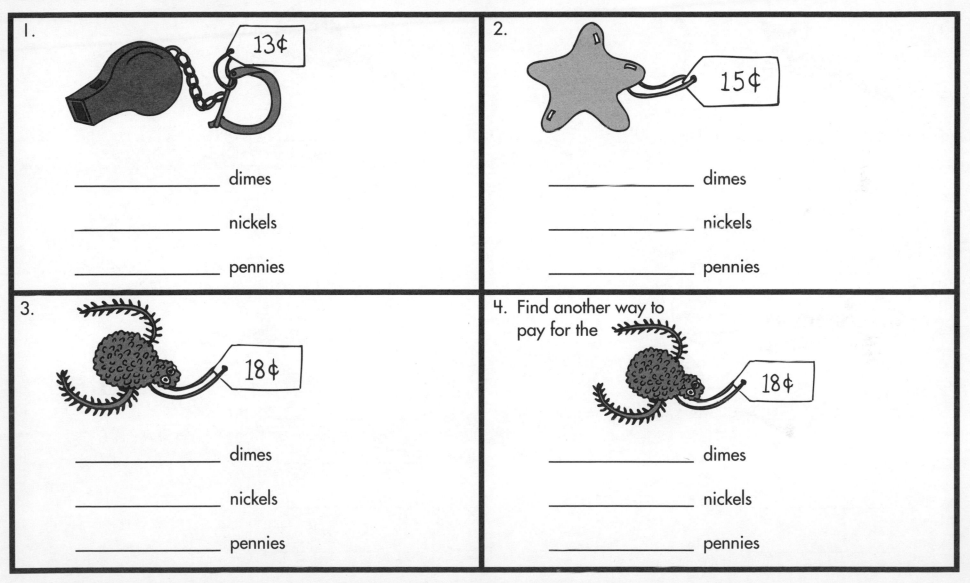

1. 13¢

_____ dimes

_____ nickels

_____ pennies

2. 15¢

_____ dimes

_____ nickels

_____ pennies

3. 18¢

_____ dimes

_____ nickels

_____ pennies

4. Find another way to pay for the 18¢

_____ dimes

_____ nickels

_____ pennies

Directions: Draw the coins you use. Write the number of coins in each blank.

Name _____

1.

50¢

_____ quarters

_____ dimes

_____ nickels

_____ pennies

2.

66¢

_____ quarters

_____ dimes

_____ nickels

_____ pennies

3.

70¢

_____ quarters

_____ dimes

_____ nickels

_____ pennies

4. Find another way to pay for the

70¢

_____ quarters

_____ dimes

_____ nickels

_____ pennies

Find two ways to pay. **Show** what coins you use.

Name _____

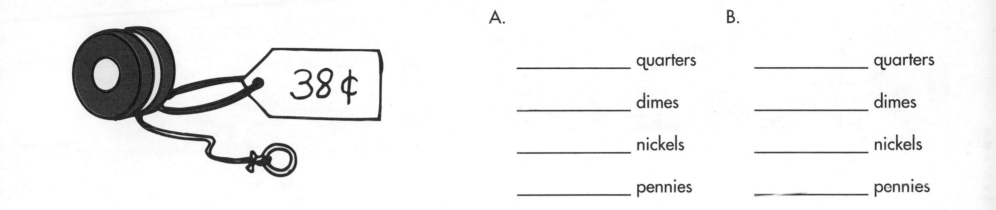

38¢

A.

_____ quarters

_____ dimes

_____ nickels

_____ pennies

B.

_____ quarters

_____ dimes

_____ nickels

_____ pennies

40¢

C.

_____ quarters

_____ dimes

_____ nickels

_____ pennies

D.

_____ quarters

_____ dimes

_____ nickels

_____ pennies

Find two ways to pay. **Show** what coins you use.

Name _____

27¢

A.

_____ quarters

_____ dimes

_____ nickels

_____ pennies

B.

_____ quarters

_____ dimes

_____ nickels

_____ pennies

32¢

C.

_____ quarters

_____ dimes

_____ nickels

_____ pennies

D.

_____ quarters

_____ dimes

_____ nickels

_____ pennies

Answer Key

Page 6

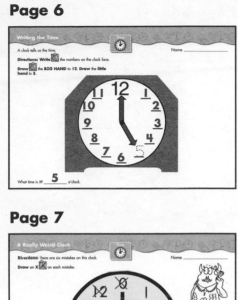

Page 7

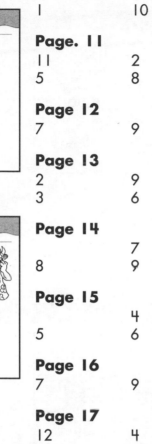

Page 9

12
8

Page 10

12	12
3	6
3	6
12	12

| 1 | 10 |
| 1 | 10 |

Page. 11

| 11 | 2 |
| 5 | 8 |

Page 12

| 7 | 9 |

Page 13

| 2 | 9 |
| 3 | 6 |

Page 14

| | 7 |
| 8 | 9 |

Page 15

| | 4 |
| 5 | 6 |

Page 16

| 7 | 9 |

Page 17

| 12 | 4 |
| 6 | 8 |

Page 18

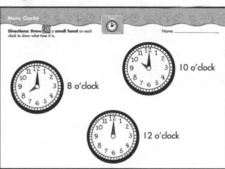

Page 19

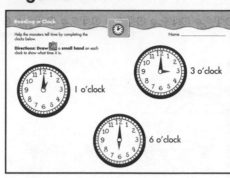

Page 20

12
10
10

Page 21

Page 22

Page 23

Page 24

Page. 25

Page 26

| 9 | 1 | 8 | 10 |
| 5 | 2 | 10 | 12 |

Page 27

| 1 | 2 | 3 |
| 1:00 | 2:00 | 3:00 |

| 4 | 5 | 6 |
| 4:00 | 5:00 | 6:00 |

| 7 | 8 | 9 |
| 7:00 | 8:00 | 9:00 |

Page 28

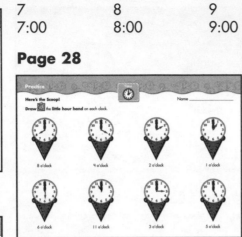

Page 29

2	12	9	1
4	11	6	8
3	5	10	7

Page 30

7	12	3
6	11	1
8	4	2

Page 31

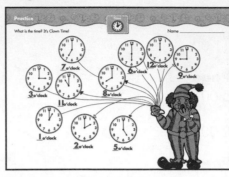

Page 32

7:00   8:00

4:00   5:00

Page 33

Page 34

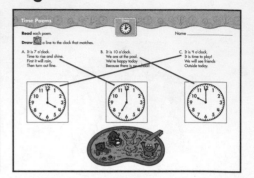

Page 35

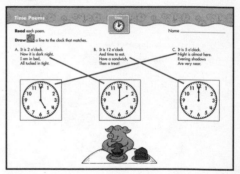

Page 36

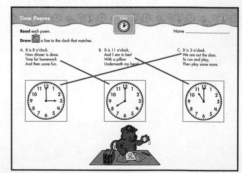

Page 37

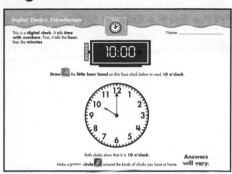

Page 38

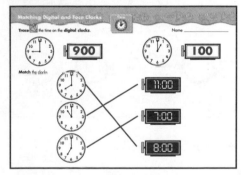

Page 39

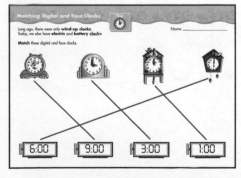

Page 40

4:00	3:00
11:00	7:00

Page 41

5:00	12:00
8:00	3:00

Page 42

2:00	10:00
6:00	1:00

Page 43

Page 44

Page 45

Page 46

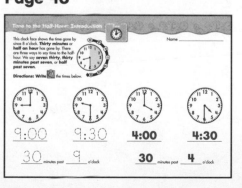

Page 47

Page 48

2	9	11
12	11	1

Page 49

9:00	9:30	2:00	2:30
5:00	5:30	8:00	8:30

Page 50

Answers will vary.

Answer Key

Page 51

Answers will vary.

Page 52
4:00   6:30   5:00

Page 53
8:00   1

10:30

10:00   9

Page 54
3:00   9:30   10:30   12:00   7:00

8:00   7:30   2:00   11:00

1:30   6:30   4:30

Page 55

4:30   10:00   3:30   1:30

9:30   4:00   2:30   7:00

Page 56

Page 57
00   05   10   15   20
25   30   35

It is 35 minutes after 7 o'clock.

7:35

Page 59

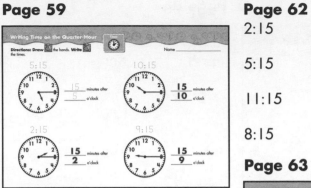

Page 60
9:00   9:15
15 minutes past 9 o'clock

4:00   4:15
15 minutes past 4 o'clock

Page 61

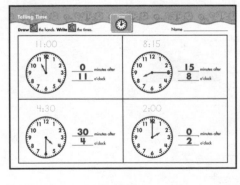

Page 62
2:15

5:15

11:15

8:15

Page 63

7:45   8:05   11:15   12:10

3:20   5:55   1:50   10:25

Page 65
5

Page 66
3 pennies = 3¢   1 penny = 1¢

5 pennies = 5¢

Page 67
2¢   3¢

5¢   6¢

Answer Key

Page 68

2¢   1¢

6¢   9¢

Page 69

4¢   3¢

5¢   8¢

Page 70

4¢

8¢

5¢

9¢

3¢

4¢

7¢

Page 71

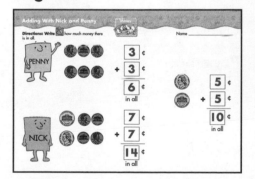

Page 72

3¢   6¢   10¢

Page 73

1 nickel = 5 pennies

1 nickel = 5 cents

1 nickel = 5¢

5¢ = 1¢ + 1¢ + 1¢ + 1¢ + 1¢

Page 74

5¢

5¢

Page 75

1 penny = 1 cent

1 penny = 1¢

1 nickel = 5 cents

1 nickel = 5¢

Page 76

3¢   15¢   7¢

4¢   10¢   17¢

Page 77

7¢

9¢

10¢

11¢

Page 78

5¢

8¢

4¢

7¢

10¢

Page 80

Page 81

20¢   10¢   40¢

30¢   35¢   25¢

15¢   45¢

Page 82

Page 83

I dime = 10 pennies

I dime = 10 cents

I dime = 10¢

Page 84

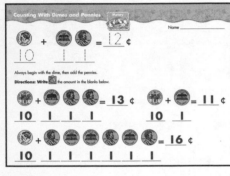

Page 85

11   13

Child 2

Page 86

        5¢

10¢   10¢

Page 87

3¢   7¢

9¢   11¢

Page 88

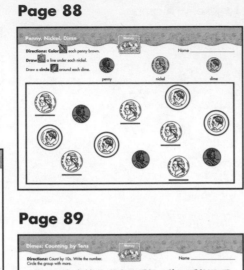

Page 89

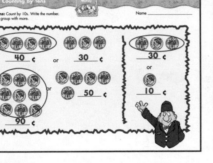

Page 91

90¢

Page 92

25¢

25¢

Page 93

9

40¢

Page 94

1¢

4¢

3¢

Page 95

Page 96

I quarter = 25 pennies

I quarter = 25 cents

I quarter = 25¢

yes

Page 97

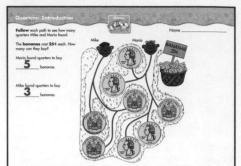

Page 98

3   1

Page 100

25¢   25¢

Page 101

45¢

40¢

Terry

Answer Key

Page 102

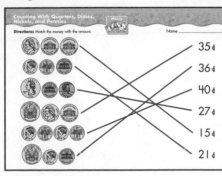

35¢
36¢
40¢
27¢
15¢
21¢

Page 103

	Quarters	Dimes	Nickels	Pennies
		1	1	2
		1	1	
		1		4
		1	1	3
			2	

Answers may vary.

Page 104

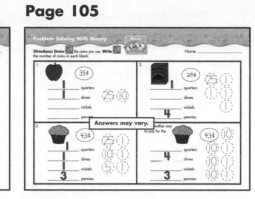

Answers may vary.

Page 105

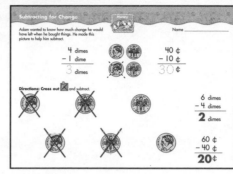

Answers may vary.

Page 106

30 ¢   40 ¢

Page 107

10   15
12   11

Answers will vary.

Page 108

4 dimes
− 1 dime
3 dimes

40 ¢
− 10 ¢
30 ¢

6 dimes
− 4 dimes
2 dimes

60 ¢
− 40 ¢
20 ¢

Page 109

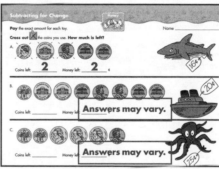

A. Coins left: 2   Money left: 2
B. **Answers may vary.**
C. **Answers may vary.**

Page 110

75¢   55¢
−60¢   −45¢
15¢   10¢

Page 111

29¢
16¢
32¢
65¢
36¢

Page 112

50¢   50¢
−16¢   −32¢
34¢   18¢

50¢   50¢
−29¢   −36¢
21¢   14¢

Page 113
Answers will vary.

Page 114
Answers will vary.

Page 115
5 pennies   5¢

1 penny   1¢

2 nickels and 3 pennies   13¢

Page 116

0 coins
0¢

15 pennies
15¢

1 quarter   25¢

Page 117
Answers will vary.

Page 118
Answers will vary.

Page 119
Answers will vary.

Page 120
Answers will vary.